TEENS IN GREECE

Teens in Greece

Greece

by Nell Musolf

Content Adviser: Yiorgos Anagnostou, Ph.D.,
Associate Professor, Modern Greek Program,
The Ohio State University

Reading Adviser: Alexa Sandmann, Ed.D.,
Professor of Literacy, College and Graduate School
of Education, Health, and Human Services,
Kent State University

Compass Point Books ◈ Minneapolis, Minnesota

Compass Point Books
151 Good Counsel Drive
P.O. Box 669
Mankato, MN 56002-0669

This book was manufactured with paper containing at least 10 percent post-consumer waste.

Editor: Robert McConnell
Page Production: Ashlee Suker
Photo Researcher: Eric Gohl
Cartographer: XNR Productions, Inc.
Library Consultant: Kathleen Baxter

Art Director: LuAnn Ascheman-Adams
Creative Director: Joe Ewest
Editorial Director: Nick Healy
Managing Editor: Catherine Neitge

Library of Congress Cataloging-in-Publication Data
Musolf, Nell.
  Teens in Greece / by Nell Musolf.
    p. cm.—(Global Connections)
  Includes index.
  ISBN 978-0-7565-4040-1 (library binding)
  1. Teenagers—Greece—Social conditions—Juvenile literature. 2. Teenagers–Greece—
  Social life and customs—Juvenile literature. 3. Greece—Social conditions—21st
  century—Juvenile literature. 4. Greece—Social life and customs—21st century—Juvenile
  literature. I.Title.
  HQ799.G9M87 2009
  305.23509495–dc22   2008035713

Visit Compass Point Books on the Internet at www.compasspointbooks.com
or e-mail your request to custserv@compasspointbooks.com

Table of Contents

Great Lakes

GREENLAND

Greenland Sea

Barents Sea

ICELAND

Norwegian Sea

FINLAND

NORWAY

SWEDEN

Baltic Sea

ESTONIA

LATVIA

LITHUANIA

BELARUS

North Sea

DENMARK

POLAND

UKRAINE

Dniep

Athens

NETH.

GERMANY

BELGIUM

LUX.

CZECH

SLOVAKIA

MOLDOVA

ROMANIA

Bla

FRA

SWITZERLAND

AUSTRIA

SLOVENIA

Danube

ANDORRA

YUGOSLAVIA

BULGARIA

MACEDONIA

ALBANIA

ITALY

ATLANTIC

PORTUGAL

SPAIN

OCEAN

GREECE

Canary Islands

MOROCCO

TUNISIA

Mediterranean Sea

WESTERN SAHARA

ALGERIA

LIBYA

MAURITANIA

MALI

SENEGAL

GAMBIA

Niger

NIGER

CHAD

L. Chad

GUINEA BISSAU

GUINEA

BURKINA

NIGERIA

SIERRA LEONE

LIBERIA

IVORY COAST

BENIN

TOGO

GHANA

SU

CENTRAL AFRICAN REPUBLIC

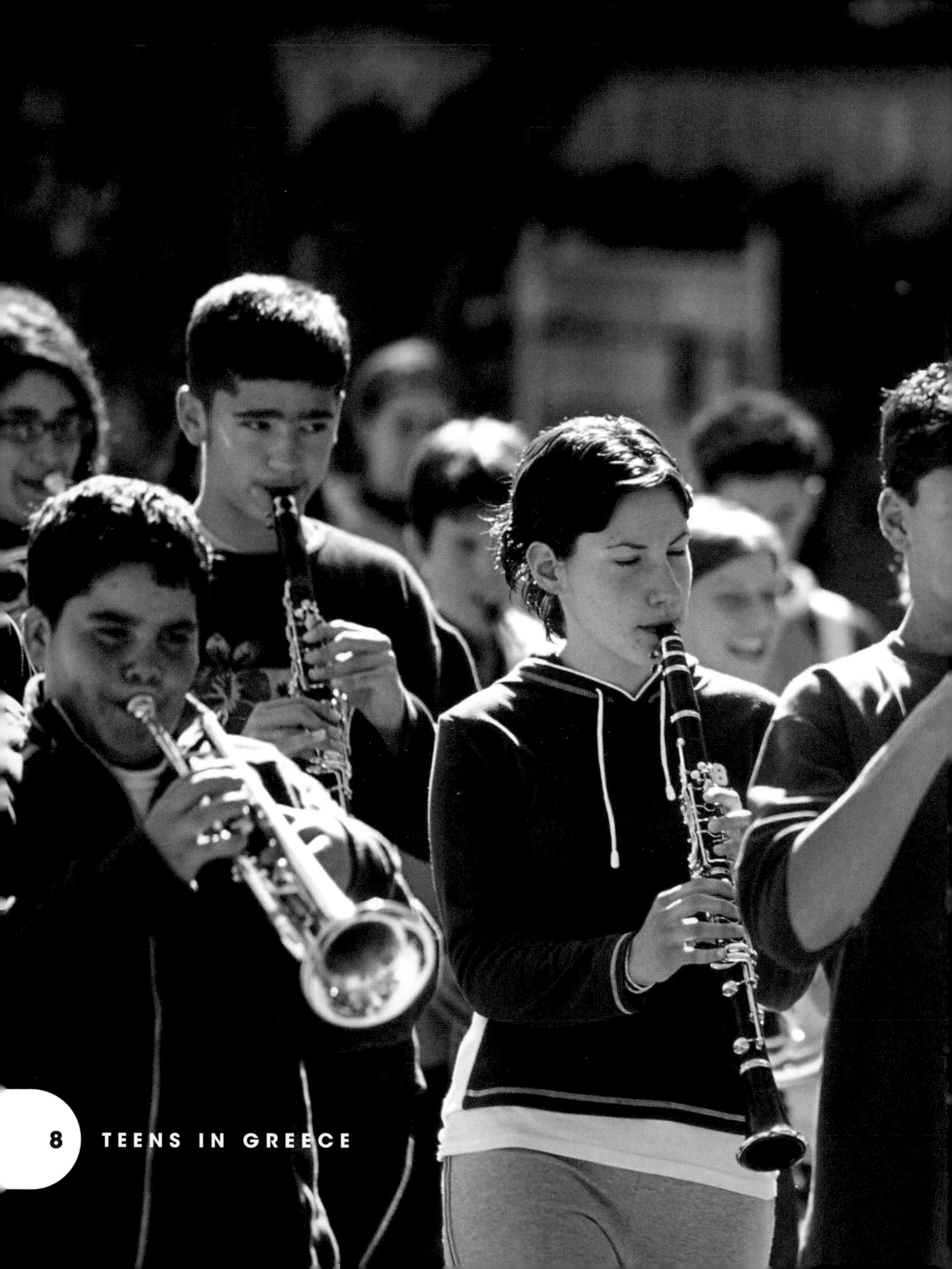

GREECE IS A COUNTRY OF OPPOSITES. Along the coastline, rock-strewn hills face bright blue water. In the capital city of Athens, ruins of ancient temples stand next to steel and glass office buildings. Air smelling like herbs fills the countryside, while the cities bake under a layer of exhaust fumes.

Teenagers in Greece live with all of these contrasts. It is a country where the ancient past constantly mixes with the present. It is also a land that is much loved by the people who call it home.

Greece is known throughout the world for having a recorded history that reaches back thousands of years. Famous philosophers, such as Aristotle and Plato, were Greek. Their works are still studied in colleges and universities. The people of Greece are proud of their heritage, and they are proud of being Greek. Greece is a country that keeps the past alive while looking toward the future.

Only 14 percent of the population in Greece is under the age of 15. That doesn't mean teens don't count, though. The family is at the heart of Greek culture, and a teen is part of his or her family's heartbeat.

Children line up outside a school in Mykonos, a Greek island in the Aegean Sea southeast of Athens.

1

A Respect for Learning

gymnasio
(him-NAH-zee-oh)

SILENCE FILLS THE CLASS-ROOM AT A MIDDLE SCHOOL, called a gymnasio, in the city of Volos. The students are studying a print of a painting at the front of the room. The room is quiet as each student tries to figure out what the artist is saying. Students study art every day in Greece. Greek teachers believe that learning about creative expression should be a big part of each student's day.

The people of Greece have always thought that education is important. Since the time of ancient Greece, about 2,500 years ago, learning has been part of everyday life. Greeks still want their children to do the best they can in school. Educators work hard to keep the country's literacy rate above 96 percent. Ensuring that children get the best education possible is a high priority for Greek families.

The First Years

Children in Greece are required to go to school from ages 6 through 15. An exception is made for those who need to leave school sooner to earn money for their families. There are preschools, but attendance is voluntary. Many families wait until a child is old enough, usually 5, to start kindergarten. The first six years after kindergarten, from ages 6 to 12, are spent in primary schools, called *dimotiko skholeio*. Primary students concentrate on basic skills—

dimotiko skholeio
(dee-moh-tee-KOH sko-LEE-oh)

reading, writing, and math. Some primary schools have longer days than others. Longer days mean teachers can teach more subjects. With an average class size of only 12, teachers have time to work with each student. When students finish primary school, they enter a gymnasio, which they attend for three years.

Moving On & Up

In middle school, students work on improving their minds. They also learn about keeping their bodies healthy.

Students learn about their country's ancient past at the Archaeological Museum at Olympia.

Students have courses in reading, writing, and math, but they also study art and social problems. They are taught to notice what is going on in the world around them. They learn how to express themselves by giving speeches and writing papers. In health courses and sports activities, teens learn to take care of their bodies.

Middle school teachers want their students to become aware of their abilities, skills, and interests. Students can find out what they like and don't like through a variety of activities. To see whether they enjoy working with small children, they might visit a preschool, play with the younger students, and help the teacher. Or they might create a budget for a small business, to understand what it is like to run one or to be an accountant. Such activities help students discover the kind of career they want to enter.

Night Shift

While most middle schools are in session during the day, a few are open at night. Night schools are for students over the age of 14 who are working full-time. Most of them have left school to earn money for their families. The jobs they find are almost always low-skilled and low-paying.

Working all day and then attending night classes isn't easy. But night school students are at school because they want to be there. Although many miss attending school with their friends,

Ancient Greek, Modern English

Several thousand English words originated from the Greek language. The word *echo* stems from the Greek word *echo*, which means "redoubled sound." *Logical* is from *logos*, "reason." *Cosmetics* comes from *kosmetikos*, "skilled in adornment." Many common English words, such as *academy*, *theater*, *hypnosis*, *idea*, and *melody*, have roots in Greek.

echo
(eh-KHO)

logos
(LOH-gos)

kosmetikos
(koz-MEH-tee-kos)

13

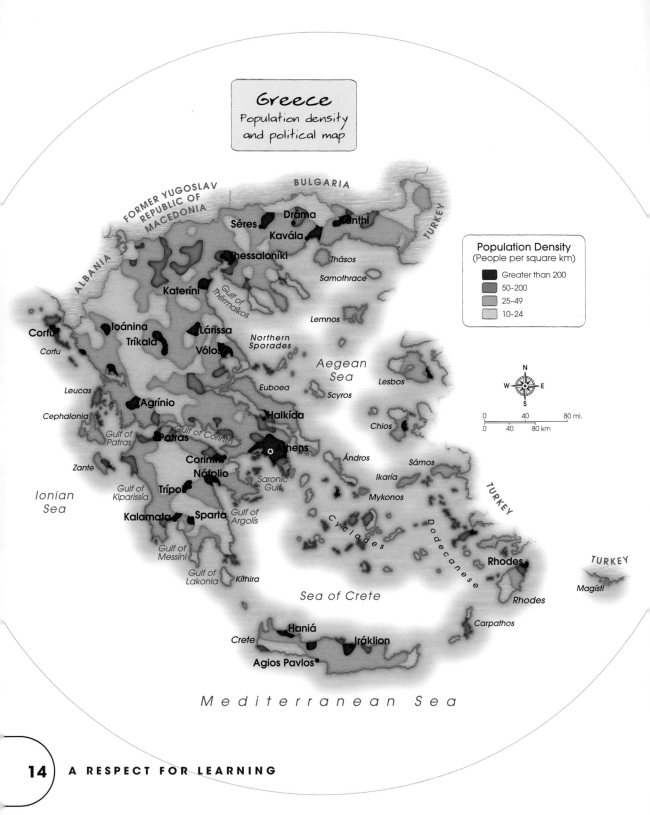

Greece
Population density
and political map

FORMER YUGOSLAV REPUBLIC OF MACEDONIA

BULGARIA

ALBANIA

TURKEY

Séres
Dráma
Xánthi
Kavála
Thessaloníki

Thásos
Samothrace

Katerini
Gulf of Thermaïkos

Lemnos

Corfu
Ioánina
Lárissa
Tríkala
Vólos

Corfu

Northern Sporades

Aegean Sea

Leucas

Cephalonia
Agrínio

Euboea
Scyros

Lesbos

Chios

Halkída

Gulf of Corinth

Gulf of Patras
Patras

Athens

Ándros

Zante
Corinth
Náfplio

Sámos
Ikaría

Ionian Sea

Trípoli
Gulf of Kiparissía

Saronic Gulf

Mykonos

Kalamata
Sparta
Gulf of Argolís

Cyclades

TURKEY

Gulf of Messíni

Dodecanese

Gulf of Lakonía
Kíthira

Rhodes

TURKEY

Sea of Crete

Rhodes

Magísti

Carpathos

Haniá
Iráklion

Crete

Agios Pavlos

Mediterranean Sea

Population Density
(People per square km)

Greater than 200
50–200
25–49
10–24

N
W E
S

0   40   80 mi.
0   40   80 km

they know that staying in school—no matter what time they have to attend classes—will mean more opportunities in the future. They might be able to go to a college or university someday. The more education they get, the better their chances for higher-paying jobs.

All middle school students have daily oral tests, short written tests, and surprise written tests. Both classwork and class participation are graded. Students are also expected to show enthusiasm in the classroom. The amount of interest a student shows is noted by the teacher.

At the end of each school year, all middle school students take written exams that they have to pass to move to the next grade. Students who don't pass must take the tests again when school begins in September. Those who fail again must repeat the grade.

Public schools in Greece are free for Greek citizens. Greece also has many private schools, but private schools charge tuition, a fee for attending. Private

For Greek middle school students, there are tests, tests, and more tests.

Teen Scenes

It's 2:45 in the afternoon, the end of another school day for a student at a gymnasio in Athens. He collects the books he'll need for his homework, puts his backpack over his shoulders, and heads for the bus stop. During his short ride home, his stomach growls as he thinks about the lunch he's going to eat before beginning his homework. When his homework is finished, he and a friend might get together to listen to music or do something else fun before dinner.

At a private school on the island of Crete, a student glances at the clock on the classroom wall. There's another hour to go before her school day is over. Leaning back against her chair, she fights a yawn. It's been a long day of studying, and the warmth of the afternoon sun is making it hard for her to pay attention. An announcement from her teacher refocuses her mind: The school is going on a field trip to a museum, the third trip of the year. The student smiles at her best friend. Field trips are always fun, and her school goes on several of them every year. She can't wait to get home and tell her family the news.

A 15-year-old boy working in a restaurant owned by his uncle also wonders what time it is. Putting down a tray of dirty dishes, he checks his watch and sees that he has a few more hours of work to go. Then it will be time for night school. Because he left school at age 14 to earn money for his widowed mother, he works during the day and goes to school at night. He dreams of completing gymnasio soon. He wants to be an electrician, but he knows he will need more education first. His mother and teachers tell him that if he tries hard enough, he can do anything.

Most Greek teens go to school at least until they are 15. But the love of learning that runs deep in almost every Greek helps most students want to learn as much as they can for as long as they can. They know that only through education will they be prepared to enter the highly competitive job market. It isn't always easy, but they know it will be worth the effort.

A RESPECT FOR LEARNING

Casual clothes are allowed at public schools in Greece.

schools have Greek students and some-times students from other countries. Unlike public schools, private schools usually require uniforms, typically dark pants or skirts, T-shirts, and jackets with the school emblem. Public school students can wear just about whatever they want, including jeans, track suits, skirts, and blouses.

Most schools in Greece start at 8:45 A.M. Classes in public primary schools end at 2:30 P.M. Middle and secondary schools finish at 2:50. Private schools usually last an hour longer than public schools to allow extra time for activities such as dance classes or chess. Students at all schools have two short breaks and one long break every day.

When school is finished for the day, many students take a school bus or

A Culture of Protest

An almost daily sight in Greece's big cities is marchers taking to the streets carrying signs, chanting protest slogans, and occasionally singing songs. They are marching to show how they feel about many things. Some march because they're angry over things such as low pay. Others march to support a cause such as changing how schools are run. Doctors, students, garbage collectors, even nuns have been in protest marches.

"This is a culture of protest," said a Greek man at a rally for students' rights. "We will defend [our right to protest] very seriously."

At the same rally was 16-year-old Polydefkis Kyriakakis. Teens occasionally skip school to join a protest that interests them. According to Kyriakakis, "It's our right to protest. The fact that we can close the city center each time there is a protest … makes it so people have to listen." Her parents allowed her to go because they also marched in protests as teenagers.

Students shout slogans at a protest rally in Athens attended by 10,000 people.

Small classes in primary schools let teachers work closely with students.

public bus home. Since Greek families don't eat dinner until 8 or 9 in the evening, students wait until the end of the school day to eat lunch. After lunch and a short break, it's time to start their homework. Greek students usually have an hour or two of homework every evening, and many also take after-school foreign language courses.

Beyond Middle School

After completing middle school, at age 15, Greek teens who want to stay in school must make a decision. They can go to a secondary school, a lyceum, or a technical-vocational school. While there are both public and private lyceums and technical-vocational schools, most students attend public secondary schools.

A lyceum prepares students for college with advanced courses in reading, mathematics, and languages. Technical-vocational schools offer such job-ori-

ented courses as electronics, construc-
tion, and hairdressing. Both lyceums
and technical-vocational schools last up
to three years, depending on the field of
study a student has chosen.

Getting to School

While school buses are available to
most students, many teens in large
cities take a public bus to school. Public
buses run often, and tickets can be
bought at kiosks near bus stops. City
dwellers also can take a taxi. Students in
Athens can use the Metro train system,
which gets people where they want to
go quickly, quietly, and cheaply. A one-
way ticket costs 0.80 euros (U.S.$1).

Students living in the country or
on a Greek island have to depend on
more old-fashioned ways of getting to
school. They might walk, ride their bikes,
or get a ride from a parent.

Off to College

After secondary school it's time for
college for many students. First they
take the national college entrance
exams. Those with the
highest scores are
admitted to college.
To prepare for these
difficult exams, many
teens attend private
schools called *frontistiria*

frontistiria
fron-tee-STEE-ree-ah

Echoing ancient Greek architecture, columns adorn a building on the campus of the University of Athens.

in addition to their regular schools. At frontistiria, they get extra help with studying for the exams. Since these schools' tuition can be high, most of their students are from upper-income families. But families with lower incomes make economic sacrifices when possible to send their children to frontistiria, too.

Greece has 16 technical schools and 22 universities. Although there are private colleges, Greek citizens pay nothing to attend public institutions. But because there are so few of them, getting into one can be hard. In 2007, about 10 percent of Greek students went to college in other countries, including Italy, Britain, France, Germany, and the United States. That option, of course, is more expensive than going to a school in Greece.

The White Mountains rise majestically behind the village of Fournes on the large Greek island of Crete.

2

From Cities to Islands

ACCORDING TO A GREEK LEGEND, WHEN GOD CREATED THE WORLD, he put all the earth through a sifter. He placed soil in one country. Then he put soil in another country, and another. When God had made sure the rest of the world had enough soil, he threw the leftover rocks and boulders from the sifter over his shoulder and made Greece.

The legend gives a realistic picture of Greece, whose rocky hills are next to sandy beaches. There are snow-covered mountains and almost tropical islands. As varied as the Greek landscape is, so are the lifestyles of the people who live there. People in the cities have very different daily lives than the people who live in the countryside.

Greek Maybe Time

Teens laugh together on a street. The summer sun is comfortably warm. Men discuss politics over cup after cup of strong, hot coffee. Women stop to talk to friends at a store. Almost whatever they are doing, Greeks seldom seem to be in a hurry to do it.

Greeks refer to "GMT,"

A relaxing game of backgammon is a good way to spend Greek Maybe Time.

initials that in English stand for Greenwich Mean Time. But the Greeks use GMT to mean Greek Maybe Time. People don't worry much about being on time, and they don't live by the clock the way much of the world does. Although Greeks are expected to arrive on time for school and medical appointments, they generally do not rush unless absolutely necessary.

Siestas are a Greek tradition. Between 3 and 5 P.M. people are expected to take a long break from work. Schools have ended for the day. Businesses reopen after 5 P.M. and stay open into the evening to make up for the time they were closed. No one makes phone calls during the siesta. In fact, such an interruption would be considered rude. So teens call their friends after 5, and sometimes late into the evening. Usually no one tells them it's too late to call.

Whether they live in cities, towns,

Where Ancient History Still Lives

On a hill covering slightly more than 10 acres (4 hectares), the ancient Greeks built a city. The hill was originally called an acropolis, a "high city" or "citadel." Today it is called the Acropolis. The city was named Athens, for Athena, the Greek goddess of wisdom. There workers built the Parthenon, an ancient temple that once held an enormous gold and ivory statue of Athena.

The Parthenon has remained standing despite earthquakes, violent storms, fires, looting, and even exploding gunpowder that Turks stored there in 1687. It still amazes builders around the world. The fact that such a big structure was built without modern machinery or tools makes the Parthenon almost incredible.

The New Acropolis Museum is next to the Acropolis. The museum is filled with more than 4,000 works of art. The nearly 131 million euro (U.S.$190 million) glass and concrete complex will allow visitors to see price-less works from ancient Greece.

Greek schoolchildren visit the Parthenon on a field trip to the Acropolis.

25

or the countryside, just about everyone follows Greek Maybe Time.

City Lights

Living in a city as large as Greece's capital city of Athens means living with constant noise. It also means round-the-clock traffic and exhaust fumes. Most of all, though, it means living with a whole lot of people.

Athens covers 158 square miles (411 square kilometers), including its suburbs and surrounding towns. In 2008, the population of the Athens metropolitan area was 3.7 million. That's about one-third of the country's entire population. Athens has many famous monuments from ancient times. It is also home to the Acropolis, one of the oldest historic sites in the world.

Thessaloniki, another large city, is on the Aegean Sea. About 1.4 million people live in its metropolitan area. As in Athens, people in Thessaloniki live in their own houses or apartments. Lower-income people often live in government-owned apartments with low rents. The apartments are usually modern and have such conveniences as refrigerators, stoves, and microwave ovens.

Along with the excitement of Athens come traffic congestion and noise.

In recent decades more and more people have chosen to live in Greece's cities instead of the country. About 65 percent of the people live in cities and larger towns. Middle- and lower-income people usually live in cities, while wealthier people often choose to live in the suburbs. As urban growth continues, problems such as pollution, overcrowding, and crime also increase.

Teens who live in the cities have a lot to do. They can go to the movies or to one of the many shopping malls. There are also amusement parks, called luna parks, with roller coasters, Ferris wheels, and other rides. Of course, there are many museums. City teens can also go to a wide variety of restaurants. If they live in Athens and are old enough, they can check out the nightlife in clubs and discos.

A luna park lights the night sky in Patras, on the Peloponnese peninsula.

27

Country Appeal

Life in the rural sections of Greece is much quieter than urban life. Teens growing up in small villages spend much of their time with family members. They also do chores. A teen in a farming family is expected to help when crops are harvested. Wheat, olives, and tobacco are common crops in Greece. Chickens and guinea fowls are typical farm animals, and shepherds are often seen in the hilly countryside with flocks of goats and sheep.

In many villages family members walk together on Sunday afternoons. Such a stroll is called a *volta*. They wave to friends and neighbors

volta
(VOHL-tuh)

A shepherd moves his flock through the mountains in Crete.

as they pass them on the street. A volta is a good way to spend time together as a family. It is also a good way to see other villagers in a relaxed setting.

In traditional villages, coffeehouses were only for men and boys, and some of these still exist. Coffeehouses are sometimes decorated with the colors of the owner's political party. Teens of both sexes hang out in modern versions of coffeehouses that cater to young people or in places that are coffeehouses by day and turn into bars at night.

While some people can't imagine living anywhere but the country, many others are leaving to go to the cities. A 2008 survey found that only 27 percent of Greece's population lives in rural areas. Many people are afraid that the smallest villages will vanish someday as older people die and younger people move away. Rural ways of life might someday disappear.

The village of Agios Pavlos, on the

Controlling Pollution

Athens is Greece's most polluted city. Thousands of cars fill the city streets every day and into the night. The air often turns brown from a combination of exhaust fumes and industrial smoke. The two pollutants create an acidic smog, which is trapped by the mountains surrounding Athens. As a result, acid rain falls on the city's buildings and statues. It damages many things, especially objects made of marble. Since many ancient monuments and sculptures in Athens are marble, finding ways to fight smog and protect the buildings and statues has become very important.

To reduce pollution in Athens, the government told drivers they only could use their cars every other day. That lowered the number of cars on the streets. But many people got around the law by buying a second car to use on their first car's "off" day. The second cars were often older models that were even more likely to pollute. Government officials wonder whether the new law is working.

island of Crete, is an example of this trend. "Agios Pavlos is totally deserted and the buildings have collapsed," said Eftyhis Sfakianakis, the village's former community president. When the last two residents of the village died, the town was left empty. A nearby village has only 61 adults and five children. Moving from rural to urban areas is a trend in many parts of the world. People usually move because jobs are easier to find in cities than in the country.

Island Dwellers

The islands surrounding the Greek mainland come in all sizes. Some are tiny, less than 1 acre (0.4 hectare) in area. Others are quite large, such as Crete, which has more than 3,000 square miles (7,800 sq km). Of the 1,400 Greek islands off the mainland, people live on about 280.

Many of the islands, such as Corfu and Crete, are popular places for tourists to visit. There are still a few that offer an escape from the rest of the world. For example, a teen living on Kalamos, a 10-square-mile (25-sq-km) island off the southern end of Greece, is surrounded by woods. There are small, isolated beaches to explore, and cars are seldom seen. Most people who live

Houses on Hold

A common sight in both the cities and countryside of Greece is unfinished houses—buildings with beams sticking out of the roofs or just stakes marking where foundations will be poured. Greeks often finish only enough of a house to meet their immediate needs.

When they need more space, they'll finish more of their home. Some people claim that leaving houses unfinished is just a way for homeowners to avoid the higher taxes they would have to pay for finished houses, but most people don't think that is the case.

on the island walk wherever they need to go.

Nightlife on the smaller islands is much more relaxed than in the cities, but it still exists. Teens might have dinner at a taverna in the town's port. Since people use boats to get to the mainland or to other islands, the port is normally the busiest spot on the island.

What's for Lunch?

Food and drink are very important to Greeks. They think of meals as times to visit with family and friends. This tradition goes back almost 3,000 years. Enjoying food and sharing it with others have always been part of living in Greece.

Greek meals use simple recipes that call for lots of tomatoes, onions,

Customers at a tavern in Crete can enjoy the food and the weather at a table on the street.

olive oil, and garlic. Cheese, fruit, and plain yogurt are also favorites. Fresh bread baked in large round loaves is always served at mealtime. Lamb is the most popular meat. Since Greece is next to the ocean, seafood such as shrimp and octopus is also popular. There is always plenty of fresh seafood. Feta, a salty, white cheese made from goat's milk, is the national cheese. When tossed with tomatoes, onions, and cucumbers, it makes what is known as a Greek salad. But don't use lettuce. A salad served with lettuce in Greece isn't considered a true Greek salad.

Greek teens enjoy good meals every day. For breakfast a teen might have coffee with a sesame-seed bagel called a *koulouri* or perhaps a *tiropita*, a cheese pie. Then it's off to school or work.

koulouri
(koo-LOO-ree)
tiropita
(tee-ROH-pee-tah)

Lunch is usually eaten after 2 in the afternoon. For lunch, a teen might

Wet Winters, Sizzling Summers

The climate in Greece is cool and damp during the winter. Summers are hot and dry. The cooler northern section sees average lows of around 46 degrees Fahrenheit (8 degrees Celsius) in January. Temperatures in the lowlands, along the coast from north to south, get down to 50 F (10 C) on average in the winter. Temperatures throughout the country usually reach 79 F (26 C) or more in the summer, with some of the islands reaching 90 F (32 C). The mountains are snowy all winter, but snow and frost are rare in the rest of the country.

spanakopita
(spah-nah-KO-pee-tah)
saganaki
(sah-ghah-NAH-kee)

have a spinach and cheese pie called *spanakopita*. Another possible choice is fried cheese known as *saganaki*. Souvlaki sandwiches (pita bread filled with meat, tomatoes, and onions, and topped with a yogurt sauce) are usually sold in fast-food restaurants.

Greeks traditionally ate the main meal of the day in the early afternoon. That's still true on Sundays, but dinner is often the main meal the rest of the week. It might include a dish such as moussaka, a casserole made of ground meat, eggplant, potatoes, and onion baked in a creamy sauce. Dessert might be fresh fruit or baklava, a honey and nut pastry. *Kadaifi*,

kadaifi
(kah-dee-FEE)

Souvlaki is a staple of Greek fast food.

another dessert, is a thin pastry filled with nuts.

For fast food, there are international chain restaurants such as McDonald's and Pizza Hut. Most teens like the traditional Greek fast food—gyros. A gyro is a pita bread sandwich made with lamb, pork, or chicken. The meat is marinated with garlic, onions, and seasonings. Then it is put into the bread and covered with onions, tomatoes, and a thick cucumber sauce. A

Baklava is a delicacy enjoyed not just in Greece, but in many parts of the world.

gyro costs about 2 euros (U.S.$3). Gyros stands are on almost every corner in Greece's larger cities.

Mind Your Manners

Table manners in Greece are not strict. But there are basic rules that all teens are expected to follow. It is normal for dinner guests to arrive a little late. When the time comes to sit down and eat, the oldest guest is always served first.

At informal get-togethers, it's all right to rest your elbows on the table. To avoid offending their host, guests are expected to eat a lot, and not refuse extra servings. They also should tell the host how much they like the food and what a good cook she is (women

A group shares the Greek tradition of making a meal a social occasion.

still do most of the cooking). It isn't unusual for close friends and relatives to eat from each other's plates. Visitors are expected to say how nice the house looks. Guests in a Greek household are usually treated so warmly that it is easy to remember to be polite in return.

Dining Together

In Greece, whole families eat together. Grandparents, grandchildren, and everyone in between sit at a table for meals. In restaurants, it is hard to find anyone eating alone. However, it has become a more common sight at places where there are a lot of tourists, since many people traveling alone eat meals by themselves.

Greeks like to pay for restaurant meals with cash instead of credit cards or checks, apparently to show their prosperity. They try to carry enough money to pay for their own meals plus those of whoever else is dining with them. It is embarrassing for them not to have enough money on hand to pay for everyone's meal.

Old and New Problems

Cigarette smoking has been part of Greek culture for many years. In 2002, it was reported that 45 percent of Greeks over the age of 15 smoked daily. This was the highest rate in the European Union.

That same year, a new law went into effect restricting smoking in most public places. Smoking was banned in

health care facilities, buses, and taxis. In restaurants smoking was limited to certain areas. But many people ignored the restrictions, so the government will put a total ban into effect by 2010. Violators will have to pay heavy fines.

A 2003 study showed a drop in

Smokers outside a coffee shop contribute to one of Greece's biggest health problems.

the number of teenage smokers. At that time 25 percent of boys ages 13 to 18 were reported to be smokers. This was a large drop from the 38 percent recorded in 1984. Girls were also smoking less in 2003, but their decrease was not as large as the boys'.

The reported use of illegal drugs has doubled in Greece since the 1980s. The largest increase has been among women. Poorer people also have been using more drugs. Marijuana is the most often used illegal drug.

Gathering for meals and other activities is very important to Greek families.

3

Close Connections

FAMILIES AND FAMILY TIES MATTER A GREAT DEAL IN GREECE. Mothers, fathers, children, cousins, and grandparents like to spend as much time as possible together. The Greek family is a strong unit. Teens enjoy spending time with their families as much as being with their friends.

With the family unit so deeply respected, divorce is not as common in Greece as it is in other parts of the world. In 2004, 15 of every 100 marriages ended in divorce. This rate is lower than those of many other countries. The United States' divorce rate

in 2004 was 50 percent and France's was 38 percent.

The legal age for marriage is 18, but most Greeks do not wed until they are older. The average age for women to marry is 24, and for men it is 29. It is unusual for grown unmarried children to move away from their parents' homes and live on their own. Young people usually remain at home even after they have finished high school and college and gotten jobs. Many of them simply have too little income to live on their own. In some parts of the country, married children and their spouses live with their parents until they can buy their own house.

Choosing a Husband or a Wife

In a small village in central Greece, a teenage girl picks olives next to her mother. They are working hard, but they are also enjoying a lively conversation about the "old days." The mother tells her daughter about how a girl's parents used to choose her future husband. The girl laughs as she tells her mother that she is happy the old days are over.

Matchmaking by parents, which was traditional for many years, is illegal today. Now it's up to the young people in Greece to choose their husband or wife. Still, getting their parents' approval is very important to them. There usually are serious discussions about it, but if the parents still disapprove, the mar-

The Gift of a Home

Traditionally Greeks gave dowries when a daughter married. This payment from the bride's family to the groom is now against the law. However, girls living in rural areas sometimes still receive a house as a wedding present from their families. This tradition began in order to make sure a girl would always have her own home.

riage probably will be off.

When a couple marries in Greece, the best man or maid of honor plays a special role. The best man is known as the *koumbaros*, and the maid of honor is the *koumbara*. The koumbaros and koumbara often become the godparents of the couple's first child. They are treated like important members of the family. In fact, there is a law in Greece that forbids marriage between a

koumbaros
(koom-BAH-rohs)
koumbara
(koom-BAH-rah)

couple's children and the children of their best man or maid of honor. Greeks consider these children to be as close as real brothers and sisters.

A bride dances energetically at a traditional Greek wedding feast.

Popular Names in Greece

Boys' Names	Girls' Names
Kostas	Panayiota
Alexander	Katerina
Petros	Kalliopi
Yiorgos	Athina
Takis	Alexandra
Lukas	Anna
Alekos	Helena
Angelos	Sophia

Fewer Babies, More Elderly

The 2001 census found that Greece's birthrate had hit a 20-year low. There were also more deaths than births. Greece has one of the lowest birthrates in the European Union. In 2008, it was estimated to be only 9.5 births per 1,000 people. It also has the highest proportion of elderly people in the EU. More than 19 percent of the population was over the age of 65 in 2008.

It's All in the Family

Greeks take care of their parents as they get older, a duty that is taken very seriously. Elderly parents might move in with their married son or daughter when they can no longer live on their own. Greek families believe that children can learn a lot from their grandparents. If a family cannot care for an elderly relative, or if an elderly person does not have a family nearby, a female immigrant is hired to provide the care.

Not Quite Equal

Probably the most important year for women's rights in Greece since 1952, when women were given the right to vote, was 1983. In that year the new Family Law went into effect. It said women could keep their birth names after marriage. It also said married people could get a divorce if they both wanted one. So-called "no fault" divorces didn't exist in Greece before then. The law also said a married woman no longer had to get her husband's permission to do things like move her children to a new home or put them in school.

In rural parts of Greece, most women are mainly wives and mothers. Their husbands go to work to earn money to support the family. Some rural women add to their family's income with an in-home business. Common jobs include working as dressmakers or hairdressers.

In the cities many married women

Always Welcome

Greeks are famous for their hospitality. Some people believe that the tradition of always welcoming strangers began centuries ago as a religious obligation. Others believe that the harsh conditions of the Greek land might have had something to do with it. People never knew when they might need help from a stranger.

Greeks continue to judge themselves by how they treat other people. They feel that if they do not put their guests' needs ahead of their own, they have hurt the honor of their ancestors and their community. However the tradition began, guests in Greek homes can expect to be treated well.

Greece's low birthrate means that one-child families might become more common.

add outside work to their duties at home. Living in cities almost always costs more than living in the country, so most urban families need extra money to meet expenses.

Wherever they live, in small villages or large cities, Greek women usually do more household chores and spend more time taking care of their children than their husbands do.

Looking Good

Both male and female teenagers in Greece like dressing in the latest styles. This is especially true in urban areas, where many shops sell fashions from all over the world. Gone are the days when a young Greek woman's style of clothing was considered a symbol of her family's honor. Girls were expected to dress modestly at all times. High-necked tops, skirts that reached the knees, and simple, dark styles were considered appropriate choices. Now, for most teenagers, just about anything goes—as long as it's stylish.

Stores in Athens offer shoppers the newest styles in clothes and accessories.

Greek women typically earn about 25 percent less than men, even when they are doing the same job. More than 50 percent of university graduates in Greece are female, but women make up just 37 percent of the country's workforce. In companies with 100 or more employees, women hold only 10 percent of high-ranking positions.

Greek women also have higher unemployment rates. The jobless rate for women is 15 percent, while the rate for men is 6.7 percent. Although Greek women have gained important rights and made significant progress in society since the mid-1900s, they still have a way to go.

Downsizing

For a long time, most Greek women didn't worry much about dieting. That began to change when television programs from other countries started appearing on Greek television. Shows such as *Charlie's Angels, Friends,* and *Beverly Hills 90210* were watched daily by thousands of young Greeks. The female stars of these shows were very thin.

Along with the foreign TV shows, an increase in advertising "created a total … change in the way people viewed themselves," said Manolis Heretakis, a media studies professor at the University of Athens. Thanks to television and printed ads showing extremely thin models, full figures were no longer popular. Instead, many Greek

teen girls and young women wanted the ultra-skinny look.

Wanting to be thin has caused a large increase in eating disorders. Some Greek teenagers have anorexia

An enormous poster advertising cosmetics dwarfs a passerby in downtown Athens.

or bulimia. "It's unfortunate that we have chosen to import the sicknesses of other societies," said Greek psychologist Michael Fakinos. Health officials are working hard to find ways to help young people deal with the new wave of unhealthful dieting practices that has come to their country.

47

The Greek Orthodox Church is a major political and cultural force in the country.

4

Keeping the Faith

ALMOST EVERYONE IN GREECE—98 PERCENT OF THE POPULATION— BELONGS TO THE GREEK ORTHODOX CHURCH, THE COUNTRY'S OFFICIAL RELIGION. Of the remaining 2 percent, 1.3 percent are Muslims, and the rest belong to other faiths.

The Greek Orthodox Church is self-governed, and it is protected by the government. Freedom of religion is guaranteed to all Greeks, but the church is intertwined with government. The government pays the salaries of the people who work for the church. By

law the president of Greece must belong to the Greek Orthodox Church. Judges also have to be Greek Orthodox. Major religious holidays, such as Easter and Christmas, are government holidays.

Although nearly all families in Greece are Greek Orthodox, some families don't go to church as much as they used to. This is especially true in urban areas, where only about 20 percent attend church regularly. In villages and rural parts of Greece, the church is still an important part of the community. Much of country life is based on the local church, which is often the village's social center.

Many rural families have a tradition of setting aside a spot in their homes to display religious icons. These images are usually gold highlighted paintings of Jesus Christ, the Virgin Mary, or a saint. Candles and bottles of holy oil are usu- ally placed with the icons. Monks make many of the icons, which are considered to be connections between heaven and Earth.

Even if a family seldom attends church, family members are still expected to follow religious customs. Baptisms, weddings, and funerals are

A Greek Orthodox priest blesses members of the new Parliament during a swearing-in ceremony.

Easter Eggs

Easter eggs play a part in the Easter celebration. Although many families dye eggs a variety of colors, Greek Orthodox tradition requires that they be just one color: a deep red, to symbolize the blood of Jesus.

Before eating the eggs, each family member chooses an egg and knocks it against someone else's egg. The egg that lasts the longest before cracking is supposed to bring good luck to its holder.

Traditional red eggs are cracked at an Easter meal.

usually held in a church. Most Greek families would not consider having such important ceremonies anywhere else. This is true whether families live in cities or in the country.

Religious Holidays

Holidays are always observed in Greece. The biggest religious holidays are Easter and Christmas. Easter, called Pascha, is the most important holiday of all. Easter-related activities begin three weeks before Lent, the 40-day period before Easter.

During Lent many Greeks fast, giving up at least meat and dairy products. Good Friday, the Friday before Easter Sunday, is a day of total fasting. On Holy Saturday the Resurrection Mass is celebrated. At midnight, a priest lights the parishioners' candles while saying, "Christ is risen." The parishioners reply, "Indeed, he has risen." After Mass, the parishioners go home for a traditional Easter meal of *magiritsa*, a soup made of lamb, egg, lemon juice, and dill. As the sun rises on Easter morning, most people go to a church service. The rest of the day is spent eating, dancing, and celebrating.

August 15 is

magiritsa
(mah-yee-REET-sah)

Greek National Holidays

New Year's Day/Feast of St. Basil—January 1

Epiphany—January 6

Independence Day—March 25

Greek Orthodox Easter—Good Friday through Easter Sunday

May Day or Labor Day—May 1

Whit Monday—Day after Pentecost (seven weeks after Easter)

Feast of Dormition—August 15

Ochi Day—October 28

Christmas—December 25

another important religious holiday, the Feast of Dormition. Also known as the Assumption of the Virgin Mary, it recalls the life and glorification of Jesus' mother. Many people spend the day making pilgrimages to the Church of Panagia Evangelistria (Our Lady of Good Tidings) on the island of Tinos. An

Religion in Greece

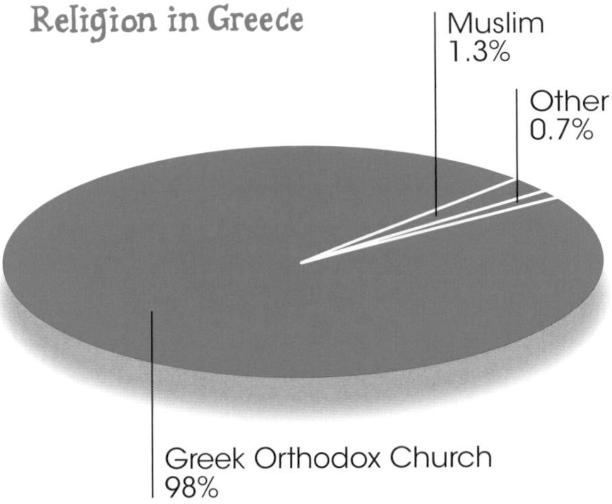

Muslim
1.3%

Other
0.7%

Greek Orthodox Church
98%

Source: United States Central Intelligence Agency.
The World Factbook—Greece

Some believers crawl to visit the icon of the Virgin Mary on Tinos.

icon there that shows Mary praying is believed to have miraculous powers of healing.

On Christmas many people have caroling parties. Then they gather for a big party. Everyone eats an extra-large holiday dinner. Special foods are prepared, such as roast lamb with potatoes, turkey stuffed with chestnuts and pine nuts, and butter cookies.

Although children might get a few presents, exchanging gifts is not a regular part of celebrating Christmas in Greece. Instead gifts are given at New Year's, a holiday dedicated to St. Basil, who started a community for monks in Greece around 370. On New Year's Eve or New Year's Day, children carry red and blue paper boats to symbolize the boat that brought St. Basil to Greece.

Another New Year's tradition involves hiding a coin in a special loaf of bread. The bread is made with cinnamon, nutmeg, and orange peel. Whoever finds the coin in a piece of bread is supposed to become wealthy.

January 6, or Epiphany, is the end of the Christmas season. On that day,

Turquoise and the "Evil Eye"

Greeks are often considered to be quite superstitious. On the Cyclades Islands, for example, furniture, doors, and church domes are painted a bright shade of turquoise. This color is supposed to stop evil spirits in their tracks.

Greeks also believe in what they call the "evil eye." This refers to a fear that someone else is envious of something the person has and is wishing the owner bad luck. To protect themselves from other people's evil eyes, people sometimes wear eye-shaped charms.

Young men rush to retrieve a cross thrown into the water by a priest during a celebration of Epiphany.

priests travel from door to door, sprinkling holy water and blessing each home for the New Year. In some towns groups of carolers follow the priests.

Towns on the coast celebrate Epiphany with an event called the Blessings of the Waters. Priests bless small boats and ships so that everyone will enjoy a prosperous new year. This event is especially important to sailors, who don't work during the 12 days from Christmas to Epiphany. All of the boats in the harbor are decorated. People walk from the church to the harbor carrying a cross. The cross is tossed into the harbor, and young men dive in after it. The one who brings it out of the water is rewarded with gifts and is believed to have good fortune in the new year. He also gets to carry the cross back to town and keep it for the rest of the year.

Other Holidays

March 25 is Greek Independence Day. In 1821, the Greeks began their war for independence from the Ottoman Empire, which had ruled Greece for almost four centuries. Independence Day is celebrated with fireworks and parades.

Ochi Day, October 28, is a holiday celebrated only in Greece. In 1940, during World War II, the Italian dictator Benito Mussolini demanded that Italian troops be allowed into Greece. The Greek prime minister, Ioannis Metaxas, said one word: "*ochi,*" which means no. War broke out between

ochi
(OH-khee)

Traditional folk dances are part of the Independence Day festivities on the Peloponnese peninsula.

Italy and Greece. To everyone's surprise, the poorly equipped Greek army managed to beat the Italians. Metaxas' one-word refusal is still celebrated by Greeks as an example of their national pride and independence.

What's in a Name (Day)?

Besides birthdays, Greeks celebrate name days. Most children are named after saints. A person's name day is the feast day of his or her patron saint.

Children are never named for their parents. Usually they are named for a grandmother or grandfather. If a family is not religious, parents sometimes choose a name for their child from the names of famous people of ancient Greece.

People celebrate their name day by passing out treats at work or school. Sometimes they have a small party. A teen having a name day might receive a call from a friend or relative wishing him or her

February 12? Your Name is Meletios

Some of the name days celebrated in Greece:

Date	Name
January 12	Tatiani
February 12	Meletios
March 5	Kononos
April 15	Leonidas
May 6	Serafim
June 2	Nikiforos
July 9	Pagratios
August 6	Sotiris
September 1	Simeon
October 4	Ierotheos
November 13	Ioannos
December 25	Christos

Source: "Greek Name Days (Eortologio)," *www.sfakia-crete.com/ sfakia-crete/greeknamedays.html* "*chronia polla,*" which means "happy many years." This is when the person with the name day usually says whether he or she is having a party—and whether the caller is invited. Teens who are invited to a name day celebration do not arrive empty-handed. It's polite to bring a small gift.

chronia polla
(kro-nee-AH POLL-ah)

Many people believe the idea of a birthday cake started in ancient Greece, when people offered cakes to the goddess of the moon. The cakes were round like a full moon, and candles made the cakes shimmer like moonlight.

Dance Fever

Most Greeks enjoy dancing. At parties it is almost guaranteed that someone will get up and start dancing. One dance closely identified with Greek culture is the *zeibekiko.* Traditionally danced by one man at a time, it is often danced today by many men sharing the same area. Occasionally a man asks the orchestra to play a particular song so he can dance by himself. When there is more than one dancer, they are very careful not to enter each other's dancing space. Women can also dance the

zeibekiko
(zey-BEH-kee-koh)

zeibekiko today.

Another well-known dance is the *kalamatianos.* While similar dances date to ancient times, the modern form of the kalamatianos gained popularity in the 19th century. Traditionally it has been danced by women, who whirl

kalamatianos
(koh-lah-mah-tee-ah-NOS)

and wave scarves over their heads, but men also dance it now. The kalamatianos is considered a national dance and is performed during national celebrations.

hasapiko
(hah-SAH-pee-koh)

The *hasapiko,* another traditional dance for males, is particularly challenging. The leader dances increasingly difficult steps. The next man must follow him exactly. By the end of the dance the men are usually worn out. For formal dance competitions, holiday celebrations, and other special occasions, the men often wear wide-sleeved white shirts, dark vests, black pants, and red scarves.

Men dance the hasapiko, a tricky dance to perform precisely.

59

A fishmonger prepares a customer's order at the central fish market in Athens.

5

All in a Day's Work

"GREEKS WORK TO LIVE, THEY DON'T LIVE TO WORK," SAID RESTAURANT OWNER MARY PAPPAS. Many of them want to balance work with the rest of their lives, but that balance is increasingly harder to find. With the cost of living rising, many Greeks work two jobs to keep up with inflation. However, finding a job, either a first or a second, can be difficult.

Looking Brighter

Greece's economy was hurt badly during World War II (1939–1945). A two-stage civil war in the 1940s, in which communists tried but failed to take over the country, was also hard on the economy. But Greece's economy has improved a great deal since 1950. In fact, in 1953, it grew faster than the economy of any other country except Japan. It kept growing for 20 years before leveling off in the 1970s.

With the help of U.S. economic aid to Europe after World War II, Greece's government was able to do many things to improve the country. The projects included building new roads, schools, and hospitals. The money also helped to create jobs.

Joining the European Union in 1981 also strengthened Greece's economy. The EU is a group of 27 European countries that cooperate to work toward common goals. They support each other politically and economically. By working together, the EU is much stronger than any of its members would be alone. The combined value of the EU's imports and exports is greater than that of any single country in the world. Belonging to the EU has helped Greece in many ways.

Visitors by the Millions

People enjoy visiting the sunny world of Greece. Going to museums, traveling to a Greek island, checking out the treasures left from ancient times—people from all over the world want to see Greece. Tourism has been good for the Greek economy. Vacationers spend a lot of money. Hotels, restaurants, shopping centers, and the economy in general have benefited from tourism.

Every year more than 14 million people visit Greece. Tourism is predicted to grow at a rate of 6.5 percent per year until at least 2016. With so many people coming to Greece, tourism is now the leading service industry. It employs 20 percent of the nation's entire workforce.

According to the Association of Greek Tourist Enterprises, "tourism is the most dynamic growth sector of the economy." Tourism brings more money into the country than any other industry in Greece. It has even passed the shipping industry, which used to be the top-earning part of the economy. However, shipping is still important. Greece has more than 1,800 merchant ships, and

The Greek Tycoon

Although Aristotle Onassis died in 1975, many people still remember the famous Greek businessman. For a long time he was one of the wealthiest men in the world. Although he was born into a poor family, he wanted to change his life. During the Great Depression of the 1930s, he bought freighters at low prices. By the end of World War II, he had built up a huge shipping fleet. He later bought hotels and banks. Eventually he owned property around the world. Onassis was also famous for another reason: In 1968 he married Jacqueline Bouvier Kennedy, the widow of former U.S. President John F. Kennedy.

Tourism is a big—and growing—business in Greece, which attracts millions of foreign visitors annually.

the shipping industry employs 4 percent of the workforce.

About 20 percent of Greek workers have jobs in manufacturing. Some make such things as beverages, cement, or chemicals. Others make clothing, processed foods, and textiles. In Athens and Thessaloniki, factories produce metals, pharmaceuticals, and rubber products.

There are few natural resources in Greece's soil. Bauxite, a metal used to make aluminum, is mined. So is lignite, a kind of coal that is burned in power plants to make electricity. Chromite, which is also mined, is a mineral used to make stainless steel.

Greece
Land Use map

FORMER YUGOSLAV REPUBLIC OF MACEDONIA

BULGARIA

ALBANIA

TURKEY

Thessaloníki

Thásos

Samothrace

Gulf of Thérmaïkos

Lárissa

Vólos

Northern Sporades

Lemnos

Aegean Sea

Corfu

Leucas

Cephalonia

Euboea

Scyros

Lesbos

Chios

Zante

Gulf of Patras

Patras

Gulf of Corinth

★ **Athens**

Saronic Gulf

Ándros

Sámos

Ikaría

Mykonos

TURKEY

Ionian Sea

Gulf of Kiparissía

Gulf of Argolís

Cyclades

Dodecanese

Gulf of Messíni

Gulf of Lakonía

Kíthira

Sea of Crete

Rhodes

TURKEY

Magísti

Carpathos

Crete

Iráklion

Mediterranean Sea

Land Use

Cropland
Forest
Livestock
Manufacturing
Tobacco
Wine and grapes

N
W E
S

0   40   80 mi.
0   40   80 km

Agricultural workers account for another 12 percent of the Greek workforce. Since Greece's land surface is about 80 percent mountains, it has little fertile land. The farms tend to be small, usually about 8 acres (3.2 hectares) in size. The most fertile areas of farmland are along the coastlines, but some good farming areas are in the interior. The mountain regions are covered with rocky soil that is poor for farming.

In most parts of the country Greek farmers use modern farming methods. Tractors, combines (harvesting machines), and trucks help farmers get their work done. Some farmers raise tomatoes, wheat, and sugar beets while others grow orange and lemon trees. Some varieties of the oranges that grow there are too bitter to be eaten raw. They are used mainly to make marmalade.

Fishing is an old Greek occupation. With more than 9,000 miles (14,500 km) of coastline on the mainland, the sea is near just about everyone. Lobster, shrimp, sardines, mackerel, and anchovies are all caught in the Aegean Sea. More than half of all the sea bass caught in the EU is from Greece. Commercial fishing is usually done in the Aegean Sea. Those who fish range from small family-sized operations with wooden boats to big businesses with large boats called trawlers. The EU has helped Greece build lagoons in which trout, carp, eels, and other fish are raised.

The Greek government controls many industries and employs about 20 percent of the total workforce. Education and the health care industry

A fisherman tends a line on a boat in the harbor of Gialos, on the island of Symi.

65

are both run by the government. Some Greeks want the government to give businesses control over certain jobs. This would save the government a lot of money. However, many like the system the way it is. They are afraid that if the government doesn't run certain industries, such as health care, the services might be too expensive for the average Greek citizen. It's a topic that a lot of people argue about.

Unemployment in Greece is about 10 percent, which is high compared with unemployment in many other countries. One of every 10 people who want a job doesn't have one. This is one of the highest unemployment rates in the EU. Portugal, for example, has an unemployment rate of about 7 percent. Austria's is about 5 percent.

The average pay for Greek workers is in about the middle of the EU scale. About 10 percent of a worker's pay in Greece goes to national health care, but the government pays for doctor visits and hospitalization. Another 10 percent goes to taxes.

Immigration Troubles

Illegal immigration has recently become a problem in Greece. As in many other countries, Greece has strict procedures for legal immigration. Generally speaking, legal immigrants must be moving to Greece for work, to reunite with a family member, or for political reasons. Many immigrants who enter Greece illegally come from Albania, Pakistan, and Russia. They want to find a better way of life.

Some employers say illegal immigrants will take jobs that many Greeks refuse to do. But many people say the illegal immigrants are using Greece's health care system, which makes the system cost more.

There is a lot of tension over how to handle the immigration situation. Some people born in Greece are especially worried about the fact that 70 percent of all births in Greece are to immigrants, both legal and illegal.

Quite a Catch

In 2006, a Greek fisherman had an unusual day at work. Pulling up his net, he found that he'd "caught" the male torso of a bronze statue. It was brought up near the island of Kalymnos in the Aegean Sea. The fisherman gave it to authorities, who discovered that it belonged to a statue of a horseback rider. It might have sunk aboard an ancient boat, probably sometime in the first century B.C.

Paycheck to Paycheck

A sampling of the monthly minimum wage:

Country	Minimum Monthly Wage
Luxembourg	1,570 euros (U.S. $2,448)
Ireland	1,403 euros (U.S. $2,187)
Greece	668 euros (U.S. $1,041)
Latvia	174 euros (U.S. $271)
Romania	114 euros (U.S. $178)
Bulgaria	92 euros (U.S. $143)

Source: Hellenic Republic Embassy of Greece

Protesting immigrants demand both a right to work and citizenship for their children born in Greece.

I WAS BORN HERE

The government is trying to find a solution to this difficult problem while being fair to everyone. As a government employee said, "Even a slight improvement of the current situation would be a great achievement."

Teens at Work

A teenager in Thessaloniki cleans the tables in his uncle's restaurant. It has been a busy day. It seems as if there has been a nonstop flow of customers. He's hot, tired, and ready to go home. Still, he knows he is lucky to have a part-time job.

A 16-year-old girl watches carefully. Her aunt is pushing a needle threaded with bright red silk into an embroidered tablecloth she is making. When it is finished, she will give it to her niece to sell at a nearby outdoor market. It is difficult work, and her aunt has been sewing for a long time. The girl thinks her aunt's sewing is a work of art. She's proud to be learning embroidery from such a fine teacher.

It's early in the morning. A young teen stands on the shore as a group of fishermen set out in their wooden boats. The air is cool and damp, but the boy doesn't notice. He can hardly wait to be old enough to become a real fisherman.

Greek teens can begin working when they are 16 years old. Younger children are allowed to work on family farms or in family-owned businesses or restaurants. There also is an exception to the minimum working age for teens younger than 16 who do artistic work. This is because Greeks believe it is important to encourage creativity in young people.

A Tough Job Hunt

Finding work in Greece is not easy. Even college graduates often have a difficult time getting hired because there are more people looking for jobs than there are jobs. Many college graduates

A Call to Duty

The government wants to make sure that Greece has a strong national defense. Neighboring countries, especially Turkey, have often not gotten along with Greece. About 165,000 people serve in Greece's army, navy, and air force. Greek men can sign up at age 18. The time they must serve depends on their branch of service. Women can volunteer for regular service, but they are given support jobs that don't involve combat.

are forced to work temporarily in a service industry until they can find a job in their field.

Since getting into college is hard in Greece, many teens, especially those from middle- or upper-income families, focus on studying for college entrance exams. They usually don't have enough time even for part-time jobs. They want to be able to go to college, earn a degree, and then find a job that is right for them.

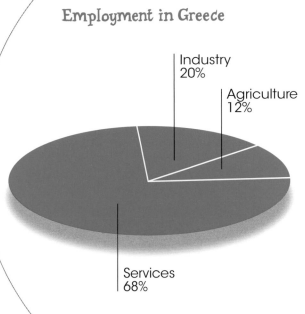

Employment in Greece

Industry 20%

Agriculture 12%

Services 68%

Source: United States Central Intelligence Agency.
The World Factbook—Greece

Literary Stars

Art and Greece have always been closely linked. Being an artist of any kind is a highly respected occupation. Creativity is admired, both within the education system and by society in general. Greece has placed great importance on the written word ever since the ancient Greek Homer, according to tradition, wrote the *Illiad* and *Odyssey*, two famous epic poems. An important 20th century Greek writer is Nikos Kazantzakis, author of *Zorba the Greek* and *The Last Temptation of Christ*, both of which were made into movies shown worldwide. Harry Mark Petrakis and Jeffrey Eugenides are both famous Greek-American novelists.

Greeks young and old enjoy simply getting together for conversation.

6

When It's Downtime

oopa
(OH-pah)

OOPA! IT'S A CRY HEARD OFTEN IN GREECE WHEN YOUNG CHILDREN, teens, and adults get together to celebrate births, weddings, holidays, or simply life in general. Oopa is really more of a sound than a word. It is used to express the deep joy of living that is found everywhere in Greece.

Let's Talk About It

Having lively conversations is a big part of being Greek. In any restaurant or coffee shop, you probably will see at least a few teens talking to each other. Most likely they will be using a lot of hand gestures, a common practice in Greece. One gesture is crossing two fingers and holding them in the air. This means a teen hopes something will happen. Pulling on an eyelid shows you don't believe something. One gesture you probably won't see is showing the palm of the hand with the fingers sticking out. That's considered an insult.

Greeks of all ages like

71

to get together and talk about anything and everything. This tradition dates to ancient times when Greek philosophers spent a lot of time having long, often serious, conversations with their friends. They discussed everything from math formulas to the basics of logic. From those long-ago conversations, the modern world gained a lot of knowledge.

It is said that in those days, Greeks would rather have been in a crowded place where they could talk with their friends than alone in someplace peaceful. Clearly that hasn't changed.

Night Life

The joy of life, and the pleasure of spending time with others, are found in Greek teens, too. It is probably a very good thing that most Greeks get a rest period during the afternoon. The nightlife in Greece, especially in Athens and other big cities, lasts until the early hours of the morning. "Athens is alive 24 hours a day," said restaurant owner Mary Pappas. Late nights give teens a lot of time to enjoy themselves on weekends and during vacations. Because of the closeness of most Greek families, parents are likely to know what their teens are doing, and they usually let them make their own schedules.

At discos, music and dancing go on almost all night. The drinking age in Greece is 16. If a young adult decides to have an alcoholic beverage, a popular choice is ouzo, a clear liquid that tastes like black licorice. It turns milky white when ice is added to it. Retsina, another frequent drink choice for young adults, is a white wine flavored with pine resin.

However, most teens prefer coffee. Their favorite way to enjoy it is as a frappé, a combination of coffee, water, sugar, and sometimes milk that is whipped and poured over ice. Adults usually drink strong regular coffee, made with plenty of grounds and boiling water. It is poured into tiny cups and sipped very slowly. Coffee is served either *glikos* (sweet), *metrios* (a little sweet), or *sketos* (unsweetened).

glikos
(GLEE-kohs)

metrios
(MEH-tree-ohs)

sketos
(SKEE-tohs)

Teens in Greece, like most teens around the world, enjoy listening to popular music. One of the most popular Greek musicians is Mihalis Hatzigiannis, a pop rock singer who has sold hundreds of thousands of CDs. Teens also like to listen to the rock music of Evanescence, Linkin Park, and HIM. Another group popular among young people is the Free Monks. They are Greek Orthodox monks who sing rock songs featuring faith-filled lyrics that warn against foreign influence. Since 2000, they've made four best-selling CDs.

The atmosphere at a nightclub on the island of Corfu is lively.

The Sporting Life

The first Olympic Games were held in Greece in 776 B.C. Before the competition began, messengers were sent to tell other countries about the start of the games. But the word *games* is a little misleading. The first Olympics consisted of only one event: a footrace. Gradually other events were added. Boxing and chariot racing were two early popular events. While the Games were going on, wars and all international conflicts, political and otherwise, were supposed to stop.

Fans cheered for the Greek women's water polo team at the Athens Olympic Games.

The modern Olympic Games are held in a different country every four years. There are summer and winter competitions. In 2004, the Olympics were once again held in Greece.

Spectator Sports

When it comes to free time, boys in Greece tend to prefer sports-watching activities. Girls might choose to study or do crafts or artwork, but many of them also enjoy spectator sports.

Soccer, called *podosphero*, is the most popular spectator sport in Greece. Some people say the only time the streets are empty is when a soccer match is on television. People often crowd into restaurants and cafés to watch a match. When the home team wins, there's always a celebration.

Basketball is the second most popular sport for Greeks to watch. In 1987, Greece won the European basketball title. Since then, basketball has grown in popularity.

Another sport widely enjoyed in Greece is automobile racing. Every year

podosphero
(poh-DOHS-fay-roh)

A television set showing the opening ceremony of the 2004 Olympic Games drew a crowd.

thousands of fans go to the Acropolis Rally. Held on the rough, rocky mountain roads surrounding Athens, it is considered by many fans to be the most challenging cross-country auto race in the world.

Recreational Sports

Greek teens like to play on and in the water. Thousands of miles of coastline provide many opportunities for windsurfing, sailing, and snorkeling. Water polo is a popular aquatic sport for both girls and boys. Scuba diving, however, is against the law except in certain highly restricted areas. This law is intended to prevent people from stealing any ancient treasures they might come

A Swedish car roars past spectators at the annual Acropolis Rally.

Greece
Topographical
map

FORMER YUGOSLAV
REPUBLIC OF
MACEDONIA

BULGARIA

Lake Prespa

Nestos River

Rhodope Mts.

Thrace

TURKEY

Evros R.

ALBANIA

Macedonia

Aliakmonas R.

Thessaloníki

Chalkidikí
Peninsula

Thásos

Samothrace

Pindus Mts.

Mt. Olympus

Gulf of
Thérmai

Lemnos

Corfu

Piniós R.

Lárissa

Northern
Sporades

Vólos

Aegean
Sea

Lesbos

Railroad

Leucas

Spercheiós R.

Lake
Trichonída

Euboea

Scyros

N
W   E
S

0   40   80 mi.
0   40   80 km

Kálamos

Achelós R.

Mt. Parnassus

Chios

Cephalonia

Gulf of
Patras

Gulf of Corinth

Patras

Athens

Andros

Sámos

Zante

Peloponnisos

Alfeós River

Saronic
Gulf

Tínos

Ikaria

Ionian
Sea

Gulf of
Kiparissía

Evrótas R.

Gulf of
Argolis

Mykonos

Cyclades Islands

Kálimnos

TURKEY

Dodecanese

Gulf of
Messenia

Gulf of
Laconia

Kythira

Sea of Crete

TURKEY

Kastelorizo

Rhodes

Carpathos

Crete

Iráklion

Mediterranean   Sea

across while under water.

With so many mountains in Greece, skiing is another popular sport. In most areas, the ski season lasts from December through March. In the higher mountains, the ski season can last into May. There are about two dozen ski resorts in Greece. The largest is Arachova, on Mount Parnassus.

Snowboarding is also popular, especially among teens.

Hiking is a fun and easy outdoor sport. Teens can hike through the Peloponnesus, a large peninsula in southern Greece that is filled with valleys and rugged mountains. Those who want something more challenging might head for the Samaria Gorge in Crete,

The challenging Samaria Gorge on the island of Crete attracts hikers.

which takes six hours to cross on foot. Fires damaged sections of the gorge's trails in 2007, but officials have been restoring them.

So Dramatic!

In ancient Greece plays taught audiences what was important to the whole society. Today any social messages are secondary. Greek teens enjoy the theater, both as actors and audience members. Drama festivals are held every year in many parts of the country. Plays written by ancient Greeks are performed at the Epidaurus Festival. They are presented in an arena that dates to the third century B.C.

Like teens in most countries, Greek teenagers enjoy watching television. Most urban households have at least one TV set, and so do many rural homes. Until the 1990s, the government ran the television industry. Now there are more than 30 television stations, both publicly and privately owned. Greece also has about 20 satellite channels, allowing Greek viewers to watch programs from around the globe.

Roll Film!

Movies are popular with Greek teens. Many theaters sell tickets through a system that saves seats for customers. The cinema section of newspapers lists "reserve numbers" for movies. Teens can ask their parents to call the theater, give a credit card number, and order their tickets. When they arrive at the theater, the tickets are waiting. No standing in line is necessary (except for popcorn).

Greek cinemas used to show movies outdoors during the summer so everyone could enjoy the warm weather. Now nearly all are shown indoors year-around. During intermission, halfway through the movie, people can decide whether they want to stay for the rest of the movie or leave and do something else.

Britain Still Has the Marbles

Greek actress Melina Mercouri was famous for her stage work, movies, and singing. Born in 1920, she served two terms as Greece's first female minister of culture, beginning in 1981. One of her goals as minister was to see the return of the Elgin Marbles to Greece. The marble sculptures were taken from Athens by Lord Elgin in the early 1800s. When Mercouri died in 1994, the sculptures had not been returned. They are still on display in Britain.

A visitor looks at some of the Elgin Marbles at the British Museum in London.

Greek teens surf the Web at an Internet café on the island of Rhodes.

Internot?

Using the Internet is not as popular in Greece as it is in many other countries. As of 2007, almost three-quarters of Greeks had never used the Internet. In fact, only 22 percent of Greek households had Internet access.

Companies that provide Internet services hope to change that. They think many people haven't been given enough information about the Internet. "Neither the local education system ... nor even the major media firms have done much" to educate consumers, said Dina Kavouni, who works for an Internet business in Greece.

But change is coming. More and more households are signing up for Internet service. Companies that offer the services believe that Greeks, especially teenagers, will start hopping on the information highway in much greater numbers.

Looking Ahead

WARM, CLOSE FAMILIES. Good friends. Excellent educations. Traditions that go back thousands of years. Natural beauty and priceless ancient buildings and artwork. It's easy to understand why Greek teens love their homeland and are proud of their heritage.

Most of them are lucky enough to be able to focus on their education. They have been given the tools they need to turn their dreams into reality. They also have been given solid support from their parents and their communities. They attend schools that value their individuality.

When the time comes for them to be in charge of their country, the teens in Greece will have to deal with such problems as illegal immigration, a low birth rate, and an increasingly polluted atmosphere. Future leaders will be asked to strengthen Greece's economy and to continue lowering the unemployment rate. None of this will be easy. But the youth of Greece will more than likely be able to tackle any challenges they encounter.

Growing up is never simple. However, growing up in the sun-drenched land of Greece makes everything, even adolescence, a little easier.

At a Glance

Official name: Hellenic Republic

Capital: Athens

People

Population: 10,722,816

Population by age group:
0–14 years: 14.3%
15–64 years: 66.6%
65 years and over: 19.1%

Life expectancy at birth: 79.52 years

Official language: Greek

Other common languages: English and French

Religions:
Greek Orthodox: 98%
Muslim: 1.3%
Other: 0.7%

Legal ages:
Alcohol consumption: 16
Driver's license: 18
Employment: 16
Leave school: 15
Marriage: 18
Military service: 18
Voting: 18

Government

Type of government: Parliamentary republic

Chief of state: President, elected by Parliament for a five-year term

Head of government: Prime minister, leader of the party that wins a plurality of the vote

Lawmaking body: Vouli ton Ellinon (Parliament), elected by popular vote

Administrative divisions: 51 prefectures and one autonomous region

Independence: 1829, from the Ottoman Empire

National symbol: Flag with nine horizontal stripes of blue alternating with white; a blue square in the upper left corner bears a white cross, symbolizing Greek Orthodoxy, the official religion

Geography

Total area: 52,776 square miles (131,940 sq km)

Climate: Temperate and mild, with wet winters and dry summers

Highest point: Mount Olympus, 9,570 feet (2,917 meters)

Lowest point: Mediterranean Sea, sea level

Major rivers: Acheloos, Aliacmon, Evros, Pinios

Major landforms: Argo-Saronic, Cyclades, Dodecanese, Ionian, Northeast Aegean, Sporades island groups, Mount Olympus, Southern Rhodope mountain range, Peloponnese peninsula

Economy

Currency: Euro

Population below poverty line: 20%

Major natural resources: Lignite, petroleum, iron ore, bauxite, lead, zinc, nickel, magnesite, marble, salt, hydropower potential

Major agricultural products: Wheat, corn, barley, sugar beets, olives, tomatoes, tobacco, potatoes, beef, dairy products, wine

Major exports: Manufactured goods, fuels, food and beverages

Major imports: Manufactured goods, foodstuffs, fuel, chemicals

Historical Timeline

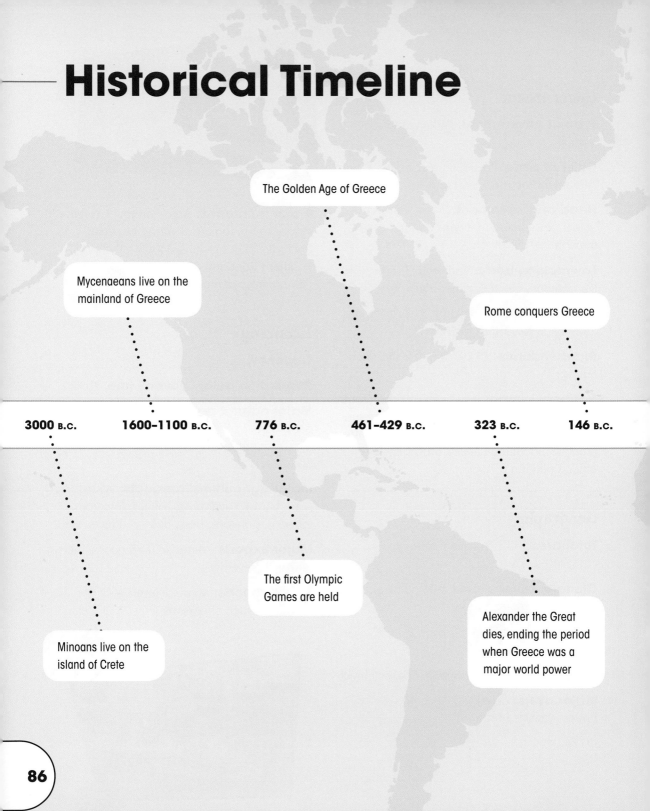

The Golden Age of Greece

Mycenaeans live on the mainland of Greece

Rome conquers Greece

| 3000 B.C. | 1600–1100 B.C. | 776 B.C. | 461–429 B.C. | 323 B.C. | 146 B.C. |

The first Olympic Games are held

Minoans live on the island of Crete

Alexander the Great dies, ending the period when Greece was a major world power

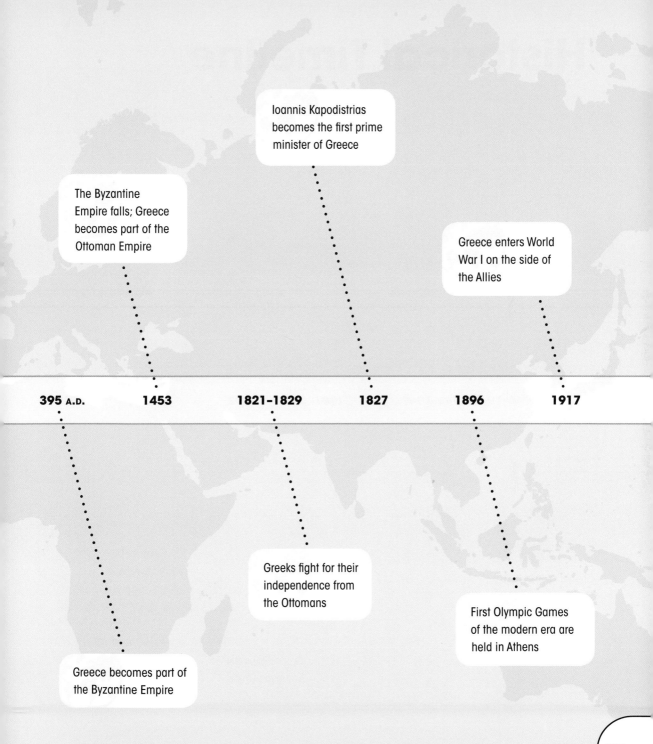

Ioannis Kapodistrias becomes the first prime minister of Greece

The Byzantine Empire falls; Greece becomes part of the Ottoman Empire

Greece enters World War I on the side of the Allies

395 A.D.   1453   1821–1829   1827   1896   1917

Greeks fight for their independence from the Ottomans

First Olympic Games of the modern era are held in Athens

Greece becomes part of the Byzantine Empire

87

Historical Timeline

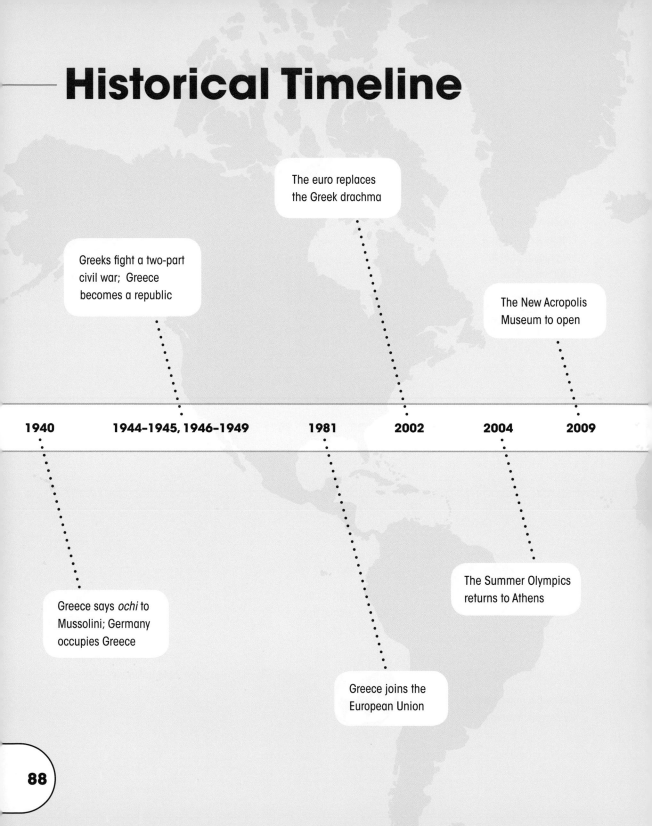

The euro replaces the Greek drachma

Greeks fight a two-part civil war; Greece becomes a republic

The New Acropolis Museum to open

| 1940 | 1944–1945, 1946–1949 | 1981 | 2002 | 2004 | 2009 |

Greece says *ochi* to Mussolini; Germany occupies Greece

The Summer Olympics returns to Athens

Greece joins the European Union

Glossary

anorexia	eating disorder characterized by extreme weight loss
bulimia	eating disorder characterized by overeating and purging
European Union	group of democratic European countries that work together for peace and prosperity
immigrant	person who enters a country to take up permanent residence
kiosks	small structures with one or more open sides; usually used to sell merchandise or services
logic	study of the principles of reasoning
pilgrimages	journeys to a holy place
torso	human body without arms, legs, or a head
tuition	price of or payment for instruction
vocational	referring to a field of employment, usually a field that requires skilled workers, such as mechanics, plumbers, or carpenters

Additional Resources

FURTHER READING

Fiction and nonfiction titles to enhance your introduction to teens in Greece, past and present.

Kimmel, Eric A. *The McElderry Book of Greek Myths*. New York: M.K. McElderry Books, 2008.

Krulik, Nancy E. *The Witch That Launched a Thousand Ships*. New York: Simon & Schuster Children's Publishing, 2002.

Lawrence, Caroline. *The Colossus of Rhodes*. New York: Roaring Brook Press, 2006.

Brown, Deni. *Eyewitness Greece*. New York: Dorling Kindersley Publishing Inc., 2007.

Cooper, Sharon Katz. *Aristotle*. Minneapolis: Compass Point Books, 2006.

DuBois, Jill. *Greece*. Tarrytown, N.Y.: Marshall Cavendish Corporation, 2003.

ON THE WEB

For more information on this topic, use FactHound.

1. Go to www.facthound.com
2. Choose your grade level.
3. Begin your search.

This book's ID number is 9780756540401

FactHound will find the best sites for you.

Look for more Global Connections books.

Teens in Argentina
Teens in Australia
Teens in Brazil
Teens in Canada
Teens in China
Teens in Cuba
Teens in Egypt
Teens in England
Teens in Finland

Teens in France
Teens in Ghana
Teens in India
Teens in Iran
Teens in Israel
Teens in Japan
Teens in Kenya
Teens in Mexico
Teens in Morocco

Teens in Nepal
Teens in Nigeria
Teens in Pakistan
Teens in Peru
Teens in the Philippines
Teens in Russia
Teens in Saudi Arabia
Teens in South Africa
Teens in South Korea

Teens in Spain
Teens in Thailand
Teens in Turkey
Teens in the U.S.A.
Teens in Venezuela
Teens in Vietnam

Source Notes

Page 18, column 2, line 1: Nicole Itano. "Backstory: In Greece, the Culture of Protest." *The Christian Science Monitor.* 29 Jan. 2007. 1 Jan. 2008. www.csmonitor.com/2007/0129/p20s01-woeu.htm

Page 18, column 2, line 9: Ibid.

Page 30, column 1, line 2: "Greek Villages Facing Slow Death." Hellenic Communication Service. 24 Jan. 2008. www.helleniccomserve.com/slowdeath.html

Page 46, column 1, line 30: Coral M. Davenport. "Greek Women Trade Aphrodite for Gaunt Model Look." *The Christian Science Monitor.* 14 Feb. 2002. 14 Jan. 2008. www.csmonitor.com/2002/0214/p10s01-woeu.htm

Page 47, column 1, line 1: Ibid.

Page 61, column 1, line 1: Kate Greenfield. "Teenagers Traveling in Greece." Real Travel Adventures. May 2006. 21 Dec. 2007. www.realtraveladventures.com/May2006/teenagers_traveling_in_greece.htm

Page 62, column 2, line 29: "World Tourism and Travel Council Study Predicts Great Increase in Greek Tourism." Hellenic Republic Embassy of Greece. 18 April 2007. 3 March 2008. www.greekembassy.org/Embassy/content/en/Article.aspx?office=3&folder=361&article=20292

Page 68, column 1, line 4: Kathy Tzilivakis. "Overhauling Immigration." Hellenic Communication Service, 3 March 2008. www.helleniccomserve.com/archivedgreeknews42.html

Page 72, column 1, line 23: "Teenagers Traveling in Greece."

Page 81, column 1, line 12: Dimitris Yannopoulos. "Greece Hits EU Internet-Use Bottom." Hellenic Communication Service. 24 Jan. 2008. www.helleniccomserve.com/.percentofgreeks.html

Pages 84–85, United States Central Intelligence Agency. *The World Factbook—Greece.* 23 Oct. 2008. https://www.cia.gov/library/publications/the-world-factbook/geos/gr.html

Select Bibliography

"Birthrate in Greece." 8 July 2008. http://search.census.gov/
search?=greece+birth+rate+2008

Curtis, Glenn E., ed. *Greece: A Country Study.* Lanham, Md.: Bernan, 1995.

Davenport, Coral M. "Greek Women Trade Aphrodite for Gaunt Model Look."
*The Christian Science Monitor.*14 Feb. 2002. 14 Jan. 2008. www.csmonitor.
com/2002/0214/p10s01-woeu.htm

Doughty, Neil. "What Kids Are Listening to in Athens." BBC Newsround.
29 Aug. 2004. 4 March 2008. http://news.bbc.co.uk/cbbcnews/hi/music/
newsid_3602000/3602590.stm

"Greece Secondary Education." Maps of World.com. 14 Feb. 2008. www.
mapsofworld.com/greece/education/secondary-education.html

"Greek Customs and Habits." Explore Crete. 23 Jan. 2008. www.explorecrete.
com/mycrete/customs/greek-customs.html

"Greek Fisherman Nets Ancient Statue." UKTV History. 10 May 2006. 29
Jan. 2008. http://uktv.co.uk/history/news/aid/569134

"Greek Government Plans to Ban Smoking by 2010." M&C Health.
25 June 2008. www.monstersandcritics.com/news/health/news/
article_1413205.php

"Greek Islands That Still Live Life at a Quieter Pace." 12 June 2007. 4
Jan. 2008. http://grhomeboy.wordpress.com/2007/06/12/greek-islands-
that-still-live-life-at-a-quieter-pace/

"Greek Life in Short." Athens Info Guide. 4 Jan. 2008.
www.athensinfoguide.com/gengreeklife.htm

"Greek Minimum Wage Earners in Top End of EU List." Hellenic
Republic Embassy of Greece. 19 June 2007. 11 March 2008.
www.greekembassy.org/embassy/Content/en/Article.aspx?office=
1&folder=924&article=20985

"Greek Name Days (Eortologio)." Skafia-Crete. 8 Jan. 2008. www.skafia-crete.com

"Greek Teens Are Still Lighting Up." Tobacco.org. 6 Sept. 2007. 26 Feb. 2008. www.tobacco.org/news/248029.html

"Greek Villages Facing Slow Death." Hellenic Communication Service. 24 Jan. 2008. www.helleniccomserve.com/slowdeath.html

Greenfield, Kate. "Teenagers Traveling in Greece." Real Travel Adventures. May 2006. 21 Dec. 2007. www.realtraveladventures.com/May2006/teenagers_traveling_in_greece.htm

Hadingham, Evan. "Unlocking Mysteries of the Parthenon." *Smithsonian*. February 2008, pp. 36-43.

Hatzis, Aristides N. "Modern Greek Society, Economy and Polity." 3 March 2008. http://jurist.law.pitt.edu/world/greececor3.htm

Hill, David. "Situation Not Greek to You and Me." 1 May 2007. 3 March 2008. http://thehill.com/index2.php?option=com_content&task=view&id=65796&pop=1&page=0&Itemid=75

Itano, Nicole. "Backstory: In Greece, the Culture of Protest." *The Christian Science Monitor*. 29 Jan. 2007. 1 Jan. 2008. www.csmonitor.com/2007/0129/p20s01-woeu.htm

"Non-U.S. Divorce Rates." 8 July 2008. www.divorceform.org/nonus.html

"Poverty Threatens 21% of Greek Population." *Crete Gazette*. 6 June 2008. www.cretegazette.com/2007-11/greece-poverty.php

"Study Highlights Role of Father in Work and Family Life." European Industrial Relations Observatory On-line. January 2007. 21 Dec. 2007. www.eurofound.europa.eu/eiro/2007/01/articles/gr0701079i.htm

"Top Surveillance Societies." *Time*. 14 Jan. 2008, p. 19.

Tzilivakis, Kathy. "Overhauling Immigration." Hellenic Communication Service. 3 March 2008. www.helleniccomserve.com/archivedgreeknews42.html

United States Central Intelligence Agency. *The World Factbook—Greece*. 23 Oct. 2008. https://www.cia.gov/library/publications/the-world-factbook/geos/gr.html

Van Haas, Gary. "The Celebration of Namedays in Greece." GoGreece.com. 19 Dec. 2007. www.gogreece.com/learn/namedays.htm

"World Tourism and Travel Council Study Predicts Great Increase in Greek Tourism." Hellenic Republic Embassy of Greece. 18 April 2007. 3 March 2008. www.greekembassy.org/Embassy/content/en/Article.aspx?office=3&folder=361&article=20292

"'Worlds of Difference': The Free Monks Rock Band." NPR. 16 Aug. 2004. 14 Jan. 2008. www.npr.org/templates/story/story.php?storyId=3853427

Xenos, Christina. "Smoking in Greece Can Cause Fines." Action on Smoking and Health. 30 Sept. 2002. 26 Feb. 2008. www.no-smoking.org/sept02/09-30-02-1.html

Yannopoulos, Dimitris. "Greece Hits EU Internet-Use Bottom." Hellenic Communication Service 24 Jan. 2008. www.helleniccomserve.com/percentofgreeks.html

Index

About the Author
Nell Musolf

Nell Musolf is a freelance writer in Mankato, Minnesota. She writes fiction and nonfiction. Her work has appeared in several magazines and newspapers. Nell holds a bachelor's degree in psychology from Northeastern Illinois University.

About the Content Adviser
Yiorgos Anagnostou

Yiorgos Anagnostou is an associate professor in the Modern Greek Program at The Ohio State University. He writes about Greek society and diaspora, particularly Greek Americans.